Autumn

By Terri DeGezelle

Consultant:
Joseph M. Moran, Ph.D.
Meteorologist
Education Program
American Meteorological Society

Bridgestone Books
an imprint of Capstone Press
Mankato, Minnesota

Bridgestone Books are published by Capstone Press
151 Good Counsel Drive, P.O. Box 669, Mankato, Minnesota 56002
http://www.capstone-press.com

Library of Congress Cataloging-in-Publication Data
DeGezelle, Terri, 1955–
 Autumn / by Terri DeGezelle.
 p. cm.—(Seasons)
 Includes bibliographical references and index.
 Contents: Autumn—Autumn temperatures—Water in autumn—Trees in autumn—
Animals in autumn—People in autumn—What causes autumn?—Why do seasons
change?—Seasons in other places—Hands on: thirsty trees.
 ISBN 0-7368-1409-4 (hardcover)
 1. Autumn—Juvenile literature. [1. Autumn.] I. Title.
QB637.7 .D44 2003
508.2—dc21   2001008756

Summary: Explains why seasons change and describes the ways trees, animals, and people
 react to autumn.

Editorial Credits
Christopher Harbo, editor; Karen Risch, product planning editor; Linda Clavel, designer
 and illustrator; Alta Schaffer, photo researcher

Photo Credits
Corbis 8, 10
Corbis Stock Market/Ariel Skelley, cover (main photo)
Diane Meyer, 6
International Stock/Phyllis Picardi, 20; Frank Grant, 21
Kay Shaw, 4
Kent & Donna Dannen, 12
Mark E. Gibson/Visuals Unlimited, 14
PhotoDisc, Inc., cover (bottom left)
RubberBall Productions, cover (top left)

Artistic Effects
Corbis; PhotoDisc; RubberBall Productions

1 2 3 4 5 6 07 06 05 04 03 02

Table of Contents

4

Autumn

Autumn is a season of change. People, plants, and animals get ready for winter. In the Northern Hemisphere, the first day of autumn is September 22 or 23. Autumn lasts three months. Fall is another name for autumn.

hemisphere
one half of Earth

Autumn Temperatures

Outdoor temperatures begin to drop in autumn. The air starts to cool. Cooler winds begin to blow. The wind blows leaves off trees. Wind also helps cool the air and the ground. Frost sometimes covers lawns and cars at night.

frost
ice crystals that form on objects in freezing weather

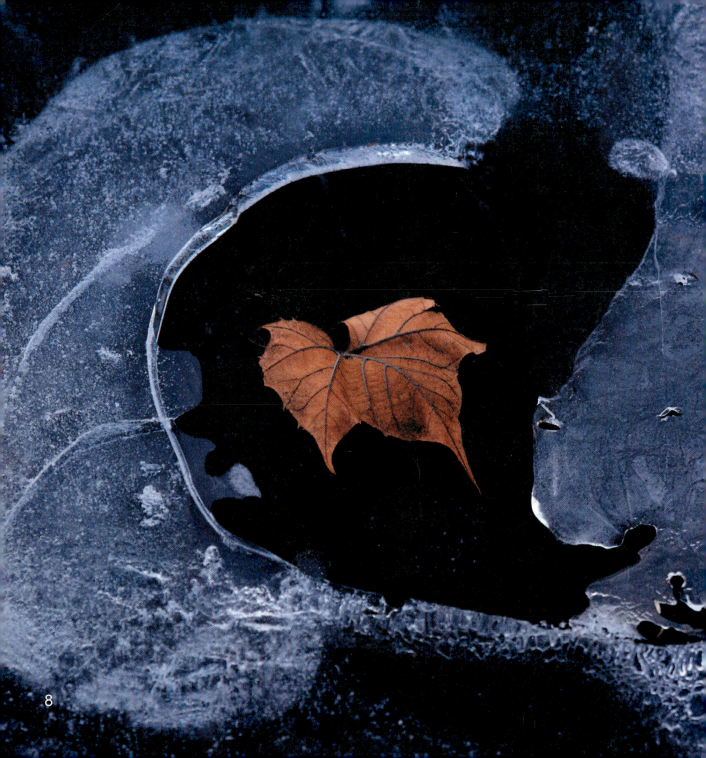

Water in Autumn

Lakes and ponds begin to freeze in autumn. Rain sometimes is mixed with sleet in the Midwest. Autumn also is the season when hurricanes form. Hurricanes form over the tropical Atlantic Ocean. They move toward the southeastern coast of the United States.

hurricane

a strong storm with high winds and heavy rains

Fun Fact

Birch and willow leaves turn yellow in autumn. White oak and sumac leaves turn red.

Trees in Autumn

Trees get ready for winter during autumn. They draw in water from the soil and store it for winter. Many trees lose their leaves in autumn. Some leaves turn yellow, orange, and red. These leaves then fall to the ground.

Fun Fact

Some scientists believe Canada geese fly in a V-shape to save energy. The V-shape helps geese cut through the air. The geese can fly farther as a group than they can by themselves.

Animals in Autumn

Animals get ready for winter in autumn. Many squirrels gather nuts. Bears gain weight to keep warm in colder weather. Other animals build warm nests and homes for winter. Some birds migrate in autumn. They fly to warm places to find food.

migrate
to move from one place to another

14

People in Autumn

In autumn, people get ready for winter. They wear long pants and sweaters to keep warm. They stack firewood into piles. Some people get their yards ready for winter. They rake leaves into piles.

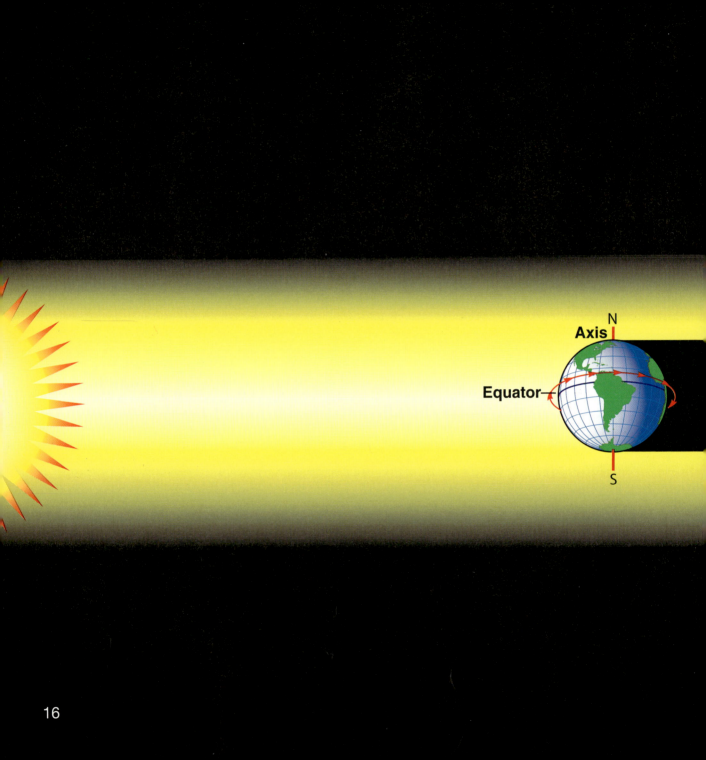

What Causes Autumn?

Seasons are caused by Earth's tilt. Earth spins like a top as it moves around the Sun. Earth spins on an axis. The axis is tilted. Autumn begins when Earth's axis starts to point away from the Sun. On the first day of autumn, the Sun's rays center on the equator.

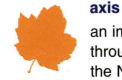

axis

an imaginary line that runs through the middle of Earth from the North Pole to the South Pole

17

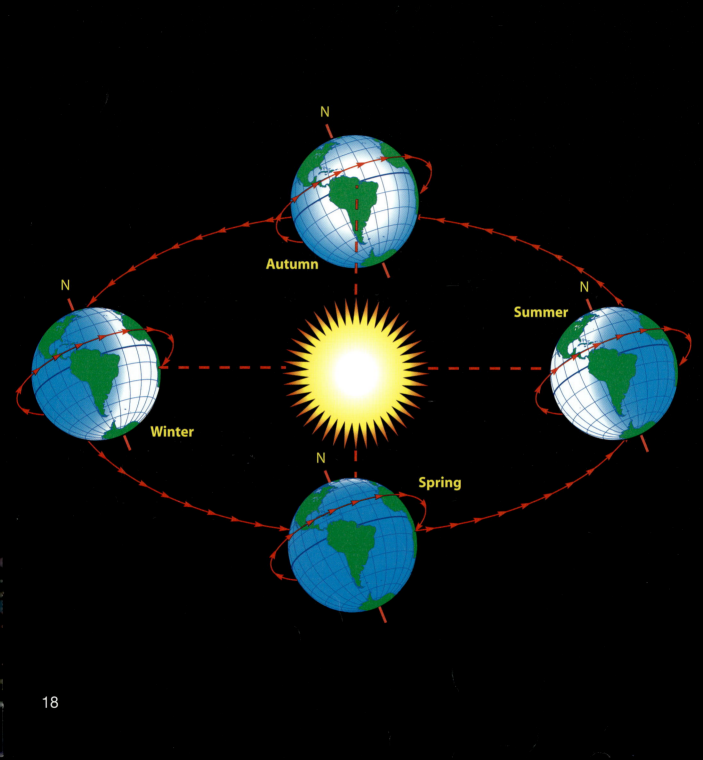

Why Do Seasons Change?

Earth travels around the Sun once each year. Earth's movement and tilt cause seasons to change. The Northern Hemisphere begins to lean away from the Sun in autumn. The Sun appears lower in the sky. Daylight is shorter in autumn than in summer.

When the Northern Hemisphere has autumn, the Southern Hemisphere has spring. Many farmers in the Northern Hemisphere harvest their crops in autumn.

At the same time of year, the Southern
Hemisphere has spring. Many farmers
begin planting their crops in September,
October, and November.

Hands On: Thirsty Trees

Trees and plants draw in water from the soil to feed their branches and leaves. In autumn, trees try to draw in enough water to last through the winter. You can see how trees and plants draw water to their leaves.

What You Need

Plastic knife

Celery stalk with leaves

Clear drinking glass

Water

Blue food coloring

What You Do

1. With a plastic knife, cut a small piece off the end of the celery stalk.
2. Fill a clear drinking glass with water.
3. Add 20 drops of blue food coloring to the water.
4. Put the celery stalk in the blue water.
5. Let the celery stand for five hours.

The celery leaves will turn blue. Like trees, celery draws in water to feed its branches and leaves. In autumn, trees need to draw in enough water to live through the winter. In winter, trees cannot draw in water because the soil is frozen.

Words to Know

axis (AK-siss)—an imaginary line that runs through the middle of Earth from the North Pole to the South Pole

equator (i-KWAY-tur)—an imaginary line halfway between the North Pole and the South Pole

frost (FRAWST)—ice crystals that form on objects in freezing weather

harvest (HAR-vist)—to collect or gather crops that are ripe

hemisphere (HEM-uhss-fihr)—one half of Earth; the Northern Hemisphere is north of the equator.

season (SEE-zuhn)—one of four parts of the year; autumn, winter, spring, and summer are seasons.

sleet (SLEET)—tiny ice particles that fall from clouds

tilt (TILT)—an angle to the left or right of center

tropical (TROP-uh-kuhl)—near the equator

Read More

Burton, Jane, and Kim Taylor. *The Nature and Science of Autumn.* Exploring the Science of Nature. Milwaukee: Gareth Stevens, 1999.

Klingel, Cynthia, and Robert B. Noyed. *Fall.* Wonder Books. Chanhassen, Minn.: Child's World, 2000.

Stille, Darlene R. *Fall.* Simply Science. Minneapolis: Compass Point Books, 2001.

Internet Sites

CBC4Kids—The Big Bang: All about Seasons
http://www.cbc4kids.ca/general/the-lab/
    big-bang/00-03-23/default.html
NasaKids—New Science: The First Day of Autumn
http://kids.msfc.nasa.gov/News/2000/
    news-autumnalequinox.asp
StormFax—Why Leaves Change Color
http://www.stormfax.com/leaves.htm

Index